# Forever Inspired COLORING BOOK

# CONFIDENT, STRONG, BEAUTIFUL, FUN

# Forever Inspired COLORING BOOK

# CONFIDENT, STRONG, BEAUTIFUL, FUN

## JOHN KURTZ

FOR YOUNG READERS

I Am Brave

I Am
Careful

I Am Caring

I Am Clever

I Am Confident

I Am Crafty

I Am Curious

I Am
Giving

I Am Growing

I Am Healthy

I Am Helpful

I Am
Imaginative

I Am

Nimble

I Am
Noble

I Am
Patient

I Am
Powerful

I Am Self-Reliant

I Am Thankful

I Am Unique

I Am
Unstoppable

# Color Bars

Use these bars to test your coloring medium and palette. Don't be afraid to try unique color combinations!

# Color Bars

Use these bars to test your coloring medium and palette. Don't be afraid to try unique color combinations!

# Color Bars

Use these bars to test your coloring medium and palette. Don't be afraid to try unique color combinations!

# Color Bars

Use these bars to test your coloring medium and palette. Don't be afraid to try unique color combinations!